Dabbling With Ducks

THOUGHTS FOR THE DAY

EDDIE ASKEW

By the same author:

A Silence and a Shouting	*Music on the Wind*
Disguises of Love	*Edge of Daylight (Memoirs)*
Many Voices One Voice	*Talking with Hedgehogs*
No Strange Land	*Unexpected Journeys*
Facing the Storm	*Love is a Wild Bird*
Breaking the Rules	*Encounters*
Cross Purposes	*Chasing the Leaves*
Slower than Butterflies	*Breaking Through*

Published by
The Leprosy Mission International
80 Windmill Road, Brentford
Middlesex TW8 0QH, United Kingdom

Edited and distributed by TLM Trading Limited
www.tlmtrading.com

*All Bible quotations are from the NEW INTERNATIONAL VERSION,
by permission of the International Bible Society.*

*Design by Creative Plus Publishing Ltd,
2nd Floor, 151 High Street, Billericay, Essex, CM12 9AB
www.creative-plus.co.uk*

Printed in China.
Lion Production Ltd/The Hanway Press Ltd.

ISBN 978-0-902731-66-0

Title page: Feeding the Geese, *watercolour*

Dedication

In memory of my beloved Barbara.

Preface

All along the backwater,
Through the rushes tall,
Ducks are a-dabbling,
Up tails all!

Ducks' tails, drakes' tails,
Yellow feet a-quiver,
Yellow bills all out of sight
Busy in the river.*

So begins Ratty's song, to be sung in the sunshine on the river bank. I thought of it as I too sat just a few metres from the river bank, looking out over an expanse of still water in the local nature reserve, watching the ducks fly in.

I'd thought Kenneth Grahame had made up the word *dabble* but no, it's a serious verb to describe a vital part of ducks' activities – feeding. Heads down, tails up, is not the ducks' comment on the state of the world, but their method of grazing on plant life below the water's surface.

In a way, that's what these thoughts are, attempts to look briefly below the surface of things, getting my head below the obvious, and to graze on what I find there. May they set your thoughts moving, dabbling, maybe even diving a little deeper.

Eddie Askew

* Ducks' Ditty, *The Wind in the Willows*, Kenneth Grahame, 1908

Ephesians 1:3

Praise be to the God and Father of our Lord Jesus Christ,
who has blessed us in the heavenly realms
with every spiritual blessing in Christ.

They came in formation, flying low across the water. I could almost hear the Dam Busters' theme playing in the background, but the noise was the Canada geese. They were honking to announce their arrival at the nature reserve and to clear the runway for landing. They came in; heads high, tails down, wings arched, and hit the water with a flurry, one after the other.

I never tire of watching them land – can you use the word 'land' when they're coming onto water? But the noise they make! Flying hooligans, big and strong and extrovert; I'm just glad they don't follow football.

One minute they're masters of the air, the next equally competent in water. And when they see the chance of food from human visitors they walk on land as well. Comfortable in all three elements. Most of us poor humans are okay on land, not-so-good in water, and the only way we can fly is by buying a ticket. Yet we have the greatest opportunity of all, to enjoy the greatest element of all – the spiritual. To open ourselves up to the imagination, to creativity, to the source which powers them all.

Lord, open my eyes, ears and mind to the wonder of your presence
and make me sensitive to your Spirit.

Overleaf:
Into the Future, *Watercolour*

I keep asking that the God of our Lord Jesus Christ,
the glorious Father, may give you the Spirit of wisdom
and revelation, so that you may know him better.

After the honking of the Canada geese, the ducks flew in, quieter, gentler. Mallards, the females smart but modest in tawny brown, although flashing – forgive the word – a small wing patch of blue and white. The males showier, lovely iridescent blue-green heads, deep-brown chest, and the blue and white on their wings too.

They fly in over the water, wings high, producing an air resistance that slows them to stalling speed. Then, they lower their undercarriage and, braced for contact, they skim the water and land with a gentle splash. Then they paddle into shallow water and suddenly upend themselves, head and shoulders under water, only the tail visible, pointing to the sky, and two pink feet paddling to stabilise the whole balancing act. Not the most elegant position.

Dabbling, it's called. I thought that was a made-up word out of a children's story – used in *The Wind in the Willows* actually – but it's a serious word used to classify ducks. They're either divers or dabblers, depending on how they look for food. Dabblers upend and graze on water plants that grow just below the surface. Divers – well, that's obvious.

Maybe we should *dabble* a bit more. Try to get below the surface of life and take hold of some of the possibilities that could open up if we just went a little bit deeper. And, who knows, maybe one day we'll be ready to dive.

Unfathomable Lord,
the deeper I dive below the surface of life,
the nearer I get to your love.

Hebrews 12:1

Therefore, since we are surrounded by such a great cloud
of witnesses, let us throw off everything that hinders and the sin
that so easily entangles, and let us run with perseverance
the race marked out for us.

When we bought our present home there was a little pond in the garden. We dug a bigger, deeper pond and put in a waterfall. We tried goldfish in the pond but they didn't last. In spite of the shelter of waterlily leaves, the heron from the nature reserve ate the fish for breakfast. We tried all the usual remedies but nothing worked; so we just kept the pond stocked with plants.

Over the years the plants got very crowded so we called in a man to clean it up and replant the pond. He did a splendid job – and incidentally his name was Mr Heron, honestly – and now the pond's lovely again. To stand there – or sit, preferably – listening to the waterfall, seeing the water clear and deep, watching the frogs and the occasional newt, is lovely. And to crown it all, we had dragonflies in the summer.

All we had to do was clear the clutter and start again. I wish I could do to my life what Mr Heron did to the pond. Clear the clutter and begin again. Maybe not as dramatically, not trying to do it all at once, but a bit at a time. Finding a little more space, more time, for the people and things that really enrich our lives.

Lord of life,
help me to distinguish the important from the urgent,
and to find the courage, just sometimes,
to say no.

Acts 2:17

*In the last days, God says, I will pour out my Spirit
on all people. Your sons and daughters will prophesy,
your young men will see visions, your old men will dream dreams.*

Milli, the dog, was barking enthusiastically. Our neighbours are very understanding but I didn't want to take advantage of that at seven o'clock in the morning. I went out, called her in – miraculously she obeyed – and then I saw the cat, the reason for Milli's barks. The cat was crouching under the hedge, her attention concentrated on something she was pawing. 'Must be a mouse,' I thought, 'or maybe a slower-than-usual squirrel'.

The cat moved as I moved but, when I looked under the hedge, the only living thing there was a dragonfly. Since the pond's been cleaned we've had gorgeous dragonflies visiting, but I've no idea how the cat caught it or held it down. The dragonfly moved, slowly – that's how I'd move if I'd been pawed by a gigantic cat – so it was still alive. I left it where it was, keeping an eye out for the cat, and hoping the dragonfly would survive. Later, when I went back it had gone.

There's always something, someone to pin us down and discourage our dreams, to say 'it's impossible', 'can't be done'. Yet it's our dreams that colour our lives with hope and give us the energy to keep going. Hang on to them, and challenge anyone who tries to dissuade you.

*Lord of my dreams,
may I always open the door for other people's dreams,
and stand aside to let them through.*

1 Timothy 6:12

Fight the good fight of the faith. Take hold of the eternal life to which you were called when you made your good confession in the presence of many witnesses.

My daughter told me a story the other day that really got under my skin – not as an irritation but a challenge.

A man died and went to heaven. After signing in and completing all the formalities, he went for a walk. He'd expected heavenly choirs and haloes, but at least the weather was good – not too hot, not too cold, just right. Going a little way down the road he met an angel. The angel greeted him cheerfully – well, you'd expect that in heaven wouldn't you? – then began to look him up and down with great interest. The angel walked all round the man, taking his time and inspecting him from every angle, and looking more and more puzzled.

"What are you doing?" asked the man, as near to irritation as anyone in heaven could be.

"Sorry," replied the angel, "I should have explained. I was looking for your wounds."

"My wounds?" said the man. "But I haven't got any wounds."

There was a long pause. Then the angel asked quietly, "But was there nothing in your world worth fighting for?"

Lord of today,
grant me the courage and strength to stand and fight
for what my heart tells me is true and good.

Overleaf:
San Giorgio Maggiore, Venice, *Watercolour*

"No," he answered, "because while you are pulling the weeds,
you may root up the wheat with them.
Let both grow together until the harvest…"

Driving down a country lane, away from heavy traffic, I pulled into a lay-by. It was just the usual rough earth parking space, but in place of a van selling hamburgers it was bordered by a lovely old hawthorn hedgerow full of wild flowers. There was Queen Anne's Lace, all cream and feminine, ranks of extrovert dandelions trying to take over everything, and bright pink campion.

Then I saw the nettles. Just standing there, waiting for me to put a hand out. "There's always a nettle among the flowers," I thought, rather cynically. Always a catch.

But there's another way of looking at it. The colour and joy of the flowers was still the same. They weren't affected. They hadn't changed. So we could turn our thoughts round and say that even in a nettle bed there are beautiful flowers. There's still colour and beauty there. It's the same situation but the way we look at it can lighten our day. As the lifestyle gurus say, "Think positive." It's not always easy but it can change our day. Let's give it a try.

Lord, when the nettles sting,
let me know the comfort of your nearness.

Psalm 5:1-2

Give ear to my words, O Lord, consider my sighing.
Listen to my cry for help, my King and my God.

I was hit by a shower of toilet rolls this morning. Fortunately not the brand that has the puppy attached. Just ordinary toilet rolls. We buy them 16 at a time – toilet rolls, not puppies – because they're cheaper that way and there's no telling when emergencies happen, which is why they're called emergencies I suppose.

We store the rolls in a wall cupboard above the doors of the fitted wardrobe in our bedroom. But when I slid open the wardrobe door looking for a clean shirt, down came the toilet tissue on my head.

"Stuff happens," as the American politician said, most of it a lot more difficult to cope with than that, and we can't really prepare ourselves for it. My immediate reaction when something unpleasant happens is to ask, "Why me?" Sometimes there is a reason. In this case I was in a hurry and just threw the rolls into the cupboard without checking whether they were safe or not, and so, later on, down they came.

But more often we can't identify a reason, and there's no point in looking for one. You just pick up the loo rolls, or whatever it was that hit you, and try to find the strength to carry on. And usually, if we've sown the seeds of friendship beforehand, we'll find there's someone who will help us pick up the fallen debris.

Lord, when life falls down on us,
thank you for the friends who help me pick up the pieces.

2 Corinthians 12:10

For when I am weak, then I am strong.

I saw something small moving across the carpet in the hall. It was just one of the many bugs and insects that crawl or fly into the house when we open up the doors and windows in summer. I don't like killing creatures unnecessarily if they're doing no harm; and when you look at them closely they're all breathtaking miracles of miniature design. I must admit I'm not so altruistic when the flying ants start but this was different. So I grabbed a bit of paper, gently picked the bug up and carried it out into the garden.

I shook the paper but the bug wouldn't let go, so I gave it an encouraging flick of the finger and away it sailed through the air. When it touched down, its legs were still moving and it crawled away without a pause as though nothing had happened.

"Wow," I thought, "if someone had thrown me through the air like that I'd be in no fit state to walk away." To me it would have been like falling off a cliff, a major disruption in my life. But the bug? Well, it just got on with the job of living. It goes with my best wishes, and I reckon it's got something to say to all of us.

Creator Lord, open my eyes to your presence in all created things,
however small, and help me learn
from their strength and perseverance.

Psalm 139:1–2

O LORD, you have searched me and you know me.
You know when I sit and when I rise;
you perceive my thoughts from afar.

When granddaughter Georgia was seven, she came up to mummy one day and asked, very earnestly, "Mum, how do I know I'm real?" Mum, not sure how to answer such serious philosophy, and playing for time, asked what she meant. "How do I know I'm not pretend?" Georgia persisted.

Now, Georgia's a great reader, way beyond her age. She's read so many children's stories, graduating from *Postman Pat*, through *Bob the Builder* to the *BFG – The Big Friendly Giant* – and on to many children's classics and more challenging stories. But Georgia knew that the people in these stories aren't real. Fairy tales, interesting but all pretend. She wanted the reality.

I reckon we're all a mixture of real and pretend. We wear masks, play roles – and not just on staff training days – often to hide our feelings, to pretend we're different, to live up to what we perceive as other people's expectations of us. And much of the time we don't even realise we're doing it. "Know thyself," said the ancient Greeks, although that's probably the most difficult person to get to know, yet it opens the door from pretend people to being real. It's worth the effort.

Lord of all wisdom,
help me drop the masks I wear, the roles I play,
and fashion me in your image.

If anyone considers himself religious
and yet does not keep a tight rein on his tongue,
he deceives himself and his religion is worthless.

My painting's been going through a bad patch. One after another, four watercolours have finished in my large waste paper basket. Very frustrating, but I carried on – the only thing to do. Giving up gets you nowhere. Then it began to come right. The next two were sort of okay. The one after that really good, by my standards anyway. Good clean colour, interesting composition, clear washes.

Next morning I kept going back to the painting looking for faults. Nothing major, but each time I thought, "I wonder – if I just added one more touch, one more brush stroke?" And that's where it can all go wrong. That extra touch can spell disaster. I've often put it on and ruined the painting, so this time I held back.

I'm trying to do it in my life too. When I'm having a difference of opinion with someone – let's be honest – an argument, it's so satisfying to have the last word. To find that cutting phrase that really hurts the other person. Satisfying but destructive. So next time, I'm going to hold back that final word, just as I'm going to resist adding another brush stroke, which would ruin the whole picture.

Help, Lord! I try to speak the gentle word,
but sometimes my words get changed between thought and delivery.

Psalm 31:14-15

*But I trust in you, O Lord; I say, "You are my God.
My times are in your hands..."*

Watching our youngest granddaughter tying her shoelaces, I marvel at how quickly children learn. Tying laces is a pretty complicated thing to do. There's a website on the Internet which proves that. It's called *Ian's Shoelaces*.

The author, Ian, has analysed the way we tie shoelace knots. He reckons there are at least 15 different ways of doing it, although most of us use the same one all the way through life.

But Ian goes further. He's invented his own knot and claims it's the fastest ever for tying shoelaces securely. Now I'm full of admiration for people with enquiring minds but I do question whether saving one and a half seconds a day is a major contribution to human civilisation. I calculate that I'd need to tie my shoelaces 70 times to cover the time this *Thought for the Day* takes to read, or 400 times to save ten minutes.

We seem obsessed by time, yet the important thing isn't about trying to save a frantic second here or there but using the time we have positively. And we forget that all of it, my time and yours, is in God's hands anyway.

*Lord of time and eternity, I don't know what today may bring,
but I know you're just around the corner. Thank you.*

Overleaf:
Market in Venice, *Watercolour*

19

Matthew 21:16

From the lips of children and infants you have ordained praise.

Granddaughter Georgia was seven. At school, her teacher sees Georgia's written work regularly – maths, creative writing, whatever – assesses it and puts her comments in the margin of her exercise books for Georgia to see. Now Georgia has a mind of her own. She decided that if teacher could write comments on Georgia's work, then Georgia could write her comments on what teacher wrote. After all, they were Georgia's exercise books.

So, when teacher wrote in the margin, 'You could do better than this,' Georgia wrote back, 'Well, I didn't understand the question.' And when she saw the words, 'Try harder,' Georgia responded with, 'I'm doing the best I can.' Fortunately, teacher saw the funny side of it, although I don't know whether the correspondence between them continued.

But I like the idea of being able to respond to the way people see us and I suggest that before we make up our minds so quickly about other people, we should give them a chance to explain themselves. Life's a two-way affair and, in our family, Georgia can teach us all something.

And that's what grandchildren are for, isn't it? To teach us new ways of looking at life.

Listening Lord, your love and patience are more than I deserve.
Help me to listen to the needs behind the words I hear today.

Genesis 1:26

Then God said, "Let us make man in our image..."

The grandchildren invaded us last weekend. Claudia, 10, Georgia, now 8. They brought their parents of course, and it was a lovely weekend. Exhausting though. They'd not been with us long before the familiar request, "Papa, can we paint?" The grandchildren, not the parents.

Off to my studio. Hide my best brushes – youthful enthusiasm and expensive sable brushes don't mix – and away they go. I disappear and leave them to it. Blessed silence. An hour later, two masterpieces are brought for us to admire. One showed a black and white cow standing in a field of buttercups, looking out of the painting with a rather indignant look on its face; the other a more developed view of Venice through a window, framed by curtains and Venetian blinds. Well, that's where Venetian blinds came from originally.

They're creative kids, but all kids are, given the chance. Children need to be encouraged, not put down. Built up, not knocked down. It can be an effort for tired parents – and grandparents – to make, but it's worth the effort. And if you keep the paints and paper handy they'll be less inclined to scribble on the kitchen walls. But even that you can put down to their creativity.

Someone once said, "If we are created in the image of the creator God, we are created creative."

Lord of all, just help me live a little closer
to the hope you have for me.

Psalm 139:14

I praise you because I am fearfully and wonderfully made;
your works are wonderful, I know that full well.

We've been watching our sugar intake recently – hope our GP's listening. We're using a sugar substitute instead. It comes in those neat little green and white containers. Hold one over the cup, press the green top, and a tiny white tablet falls in. But the other day when I pressed it, nothing happened. It was empty. I shook it to make sure then, without thinking, I dumped it in the rubbish bin.

A moment later, I said to myself, "I wonder how it works?" I retrieved it. It took a bit of probing to find out how to open it up, but I managed it. And what a surprise. Only four components and that included just one moving part. A little thing we all take for granted, using it without thinking, and dumping it when it's empty. I'm no engineer, but to me the design was amazing – a cylinder, a base, a top and a little lever. So intricate, but so simple. The intelligence of the men or women who'd designed it was breathtaking.

And if that's amazing, take it one step back and think about the intelligence of the power who created men and women with the capacity to design such things for themselves. The intelligence many of us call God.

Lord of the imagination, I'm breathless at the wonder
of the world you created, and all the people in it.
May I never undervalue it or them.

Hebrews 13:1–2

Keep on loving each other as brothers.
Do not forget to entertain strangers,
for by so doing some people have entertained angels
without knowing it.

An old friend's just visited us. Two, actually. A doctor and his wife. We worked together years ago. I'd been in India, he in Nepal, both of us involved in leprosy control work. Since then we'd both continued the same work for 30 years or more, me from the UK, he from his base in Japan, raising funds, and advising the World Health Organisation.

Did I say Japan? Yes, you see both he and his wife are Japanese. It's a long way, and very different, from the racial stereotypes some older folk hold in their minds from the history and memories of World War Two, and gung-ho movies at the cinema. But this couple have spent their whole adult lives in quiet, unselfish and devoted service to people in need.

Before they came to see us, they'd been in London for a conference and they used their only free day to take the train to Nottingham and back to spend just an hour in our home. That's friendship, and another lovely memory of two Japanese friends who love their neighbours and spend their lives putting it into practice. Something I can keep in mind when I think about Japan and its people.

Merciful Lord, may I be slow to judge and quick to love.

Overleaf:
Flower Market, *Watercolour*

Galatians 6:10

Therefore, as we have opportunity, let us do good to all people,
especially to those who belong to the family of believers.

As I walk to our front door, I look at the flower bed. It's a circular bed and in the centre is a tree peony. Not much to see now, just a few gnarled, rough stems with one or two shrivelled brown leaves hanging from them. All waiting for winter.

Way back in Spring it had a bouquet of extrovert pink flowers, each one as big as a dinner plate – well, a small dinner plate. When the blooms were at their best I said to myself, "I must get a photo of them." But I was always busy doing something else, hands full of shopping, garaging the car, or searching my pockets for the door key, or...whatever. "Later," I thought, "I'll do it later." But yes, you've guessed it, I never got round to it. Those lovely petals began to droop and fade and fall, and the chance was gone.

Not very important really, but translate it into life situations. Folk we know who could do with that bit of encouragement, friends who need a little reassurance, maybe just a sympathetic silence that shows we care. Don't put it off. Do it now. Today. Take the risk of the occasional rebuff. It's worth it. We can't show our love tomorrow, or yesterday, only today.

Lord of today, the only time to show my love for you
and for my neighbour.

Matthew 6:28–30

"See how the lilies of the field grow. They do not labour or spin.
Yet I tell you that not even Solomon in all his splendour was
dressed like one of these. If that is how God clothes the grass of the
field, which is here today and tomorrow is thrown into the fire,
will he not much more clothe you, O you of little faith."

Another cold winter morning, and not many smiles about. I walked through the echoing concrete tunnel under the road from the car park. Halfway down there was a door. 'Emergency Exit' it said and, underneath, 'This Door Is Alarmed'. "Well, me too," I thought, alone and with no-one else in sight.

But then, as I emerged safely into the light at the other end of the tunnel, the first thing I saw was a flower stall. The flowers were gorgeous, bucketfuls of colour, a whole live rainbow just standing there to lift my spirits. It may have been a struggle to grow them, although they've probably been reared under acres of heated glass in Holland or flown in from Kenya, but they were singing a song without words. A song about the beauty of life and creation.

It's so easy in these dark, dull days to concentrate on the negative – and some folk honestly can't help it and deserve our sympathy – but as I walk around with my own problems, I try to catch a bit of that colour and beauty, most of it unexpected, that adds a little cheer to the day. Thank God for it.

Gracious Lord, your presence colours my life with joy;
and when clouds gather, help me hold your beauty close.

Therefore let us stop passing judgement on one another.
Instead, make up your mind not to put any stumbling-block
or obstacle in your brother's way.

I need a new blind for the window in my studio. It's a big window. The blind's not broken, but it's been in place about 15 years and it's very dusty and badly marked. I'd rather paint another picture than spend time dusting, although dust isn't the major problem.

The trouble is all the paint splashed on the blind. I keep my palette near the window and when I'm absorbed in what I'm doing paint gets everywhere. I reckon the blind might qualify as an abstract painting in its own right. Turner Prize here I come.

The blind is – was – white to reflect light into the room, but it only does that when the slats are at a particular angle. And that's achieved by a gentle pull on a string. If you pull too hard it does just the opposite. It cuts out the light and I'm left in near darkness.

Our minds seem to work like that. Feed in thoughts of someone we don't like, or disagree with, or some situation that makes us feel uncomfortable, and our prejudices pull a little string and click, our mental shutter comes down fast. Can't see, won't see. Yet if we take a deep breath and keep the blind open, the light comes in and we catch a glimpse of a whole, beautiful world out there.

Lord of all, open my eyes to your love
and help me see you in those I rush to judge.

*But the fruit of the Spirit is love, joy, peace, patience, kindness,
goodness, faithfulness, gentleness and self-control.
Against such things there is no law.*

I have a problem with first-class and second-class mail. Don't we all. That's sending, not receiving. Mrs Bucket, or should I say Mrs Bouquet, in the sitcom *Keeping Up Appearances*, told the long-suffering postman he should only put letters with first-class stamps through her letterbox.

When I reply to a letter – thank the Lord for e-mail, no stamp required – I have to decide which stamp to use. Very often there's nothing urgent in my reply so second-class would do, but how will the receiver feel? Second-class implies that I judge a letter to them isn't important and that delay doesn't matter.

Truthfully it doesn't, but I don't want the reader to think I don't care for their letter, or for them. And I end up sending it first-class. At least it says something about the way I feel, that in all our contacts, mail, e-mail, text or just plain talking – and I do hope talking doesn't become completely out of date – it's important to treat people in a way that makes them feel good.

A Japanese colleague once told me that when he got an important letter he never replied to it immediately as that would imply he didn't think carefully about it. He would keep it two or three days before answering to show he'd taken time to give a thoughtful reply. Different cultures, different style, but all with the same aims.

*Lord, when you seem slow in answering me,
let me see it's because the time's not right.*

Ephesians 4:15

*Instead, speaking the truth in love, we will in all things
grow up into him who is the Head, that is, Christ.*

The shortest way between two points is a straight line – unless you live in the deep rain forest in New Guinea, which is so thick it's hardly possible to walk in a straight line. Large trees get in the way, and local people have little idea of the concept.

But our dog, Milli, believes in the idea, particularly indoors. In strategic places in our sitting room are small occasional tables – a nest of tables, smaller ones fitting under the larger. They're past their sell-by-date really, we bought them years ago, and they're a bit rickety. But if a table's in Milli's way she walks straight through it.

That's okay if it's the largest, there's room for her to get through underneath, and there are usually a couple of heavy books on top which keeps it stable. But when she walks under a smaller table she upends it and takes it with her. Make sure you're holding your coffee mug at the time.

A straight line between two points isn't necessarily the best when it comes to talking either. Tact and kindness may be preferable to blunt disagreement. Wrong words can upset the apple cart, or the occasional table. Some folk say that with straight words at least we know exactly where we are with people – but it's not necessarily where we want to be.

*Gentle Lord, help me to think before I speak,
and then say little.*

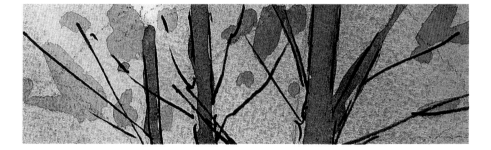

Deuteronomy 2:7

The Lord your God has blessed you
in all the work of your hands.

Catalogues. Every day they come through the letter box. Cut-price diamonds, perfume guaranteed to make your love life perfect and...well not quite. More often it's offers of corduroy trousers with a patented fastener that lets the waist out an extra two or three inches – could be useful that. Or cottage holidays and blinds to keep cool the conservatory you were persuaded to build to give you an extra room in which you'll always be warm.

Inventions for the kitchen, DIY gadgets for all. I picked up a catalogue from a nursery – plants not children – and 'spoilt for choice' was the phrase that came to mind. There were bulbs, daffodils, tulips, in dozens of varieties. Different shapes, sizes, colours. My first reaction was to ask if we needed all this variety. Wasn't the basic shape good enough?

We never seem to be satisfied with what we've got. And not just flower bulbs. Wherever we look when someone designs or builds or breeds something, others take it and use it as a starting point for another variation.

But really that's a blessing isn't it? It's human, or divine, creativity at work. Nature's always been at it, and we humans have something, some gene in our make-up, that makes us want to explore, break new ground and push out the boundaries. Thank God for it.

*Adventuring Lord, Grant me the courage
to move beyond my little certainties,
knowing that wherever I go you are there, ahead of me.*

Overleaf:
Quiet Day, Cromer, *Watercolour*

33

Just as each of us has one body with many members, and these members do not all have the same function, so in Christ we who are many form one body, and each member belongs to all the others. We have different gifts, according to the grace given us.

I love seashells. They're scattered all over our house, although more in the bathroom than anywhere else – I hope they feel at home there with all that water. I've bought a few, net bags of small and pretty shells on seaside promenades, but the bigger and impressive ones I've collected myself.

My work took me all over the world. I've shells I found on isolated beaches in Africa, in Indonesia and Papua New Guinea – places where it's all blue sea, white sand, coconut palms, and no tourists. Packing could be a problem. I've given away good shirts to make room for a special shell.

I'm not terribly interested in naming or classifying them; it's the diversity, the fantastic beauty of shape and pattern and colour that grabs me. The whorls and cones and spikes, differences that make each one unique. And when we think of the animals who not only lived in them but made them, it all adds to the wonderful variety of nature.

And diversity is important whether it's seashells or humans. Although when it comes to humans, we expect people, especially those who enter our local communities from outside, to conform to the way we do things. Yet it's the differences that make up the wonder of life. Accept and rejoice in our differences. It makes us all richer, and makes the world a better place.

Lord of surprises, help me rejoice in difference.
After all, you made it.

1 Thessalonians 5:11

Therefore encourage one another and build each other up, just as in fact you are doing.

End of term, and it's time for school reports. Thankfully, I'm way past that, and our daughters are well past it too. So now it's the grandchildren's turn. Georgia – yes, you've heard of her before – is eight years old now and is a very upfront character. Very different from her elder sister, Claudia, who has an equally enquiring mind but is happiest curled up with a book way beyond her reading age.

Their school reports were both very good and encouraging, their mum told me on the phone, but one little comment caught our attention. Her class teacher had written, "Georgia is orally enthusiastic." Well, that's a nice way of saying that Georgia talks a lot – a fact we can confirm from personal experience – but I enjoyed the appreciative feel of the words her teacher used. From being a criticism, as it might have been, the teacher had turned it into a more positive comment, with a bit of humour.

I wish all criticism and observation of our lives and characters could be made in that sort of mould, and then maybe something good could come out of it. And there's no point in waiting for others to begin the process. We can start with ourselves. Whenever we have something to say, any observation about a friend, let's make it appreciative rather than critical.

An artist once said, "Nobody ever put up a statue to a critic."

Encouraging Lord, teach me the quiet word, the helpful word, the word that builds and strengthens those who hear.

Psalm 29:11

The LORD gives strength to his people;
the LORD blesses his people with peace.

You remember Milli? Our small black and tan Cavalier spaniel. She's grown now, and recently our daughter's dog, Toby, was left with us while the family were on holiday in France. Toby is big, black, hairy, and hungry. He came with enough food for two weeks – which would've lasted Milli months – and his bed.

His bed's large, and he just fits in. A doggy king-size you might say. When Toby had been with us for a couple of days, we went shopping. We left Milli and Toby together in the kitchen. Coming back an hour later, we found both dogs asleep. Big Toby was stretched out on the cold unyielding floor tiles, little Milli was very comfortably asleep in Toby's bed. She'd taken over.

She looked even smaller than usual curled up in a corner of the bed, but as she opened her eyes I thought I saw a look of triumph in them. She'd made his bed her territory. You don't have to be large to win. You can be small and successful. And, being a real gentleman, Toby hadn't tried to get into bed with her without an invitation.

Lord of little things,
I thank you that living in your strength
brings little victories each day
– if only I'll let them happen.

First go and be reconciled to your brother;
then come and offer your gift.

It's the little things that matter, says the proverb. Yes, and small things can grow and get out of proportion if we don't deal with them. A recent report said that thousands of lampposts across the country are weak and need replacing. The reason? Dogs. Male dogs to be specific.

Yes, you've guessed it. Apparently, when male dogs lift their legs to mark their territory, the acid in what they leave on the lamppost begins to corrode both the concrete and the iron reinforcing rods. In time, and many dogs later, the posts weaken and eventually become a danger. Female dogs, like our Milli, are much better behaved.

So small things do matter, but it's so easy to put them off. We don't want to face the person we had a disagreement with, or write the letter we ought to write but are struggling to find the right words. The bigger the problem grows, and the longer we leave it, the harder it gets to put right.

Our worries may not bring lampposts down, but it's better to face things, not by using acid comments, but by making a real attempt to get back on track with the one we've disagreed with. Maybe the not-quite-so-new year's a good time to try.

Lord of paradox, remind me that I can only be right
with my neighbour when I'm right with you,
and only right with you when I'm right with my neighbour.

"My command is this: love each other as I have loved you."

I was reading the newspaper after breakfast. The news wasn't much different from yesterday's, but I read on. More reports of hate and violence from around the world, and yet more details of the movements and contacts of the London bombers. Not a very positive start to the day. It's more than enough to unsettle your bran flakes.

But there was some shopping to do. I checked my list. It was all very practical. Hoover bags, a replacement bulb for the torch, sticky parcel tape, and two kinds of glue for projects I'm involved in. "Aah," I thought, "it'll take more than glue and parcel tape to hold our world together."

But as I walked along Beeston High Street a man came towards me carrying a child. He was in his early thirties, the little girl about two, blonde and beautiful. I've no idea who they were, and I'll probably never see them again, but as we got near each other the man suddenly turned his head slightly and looked at his daughter. I can't describe his expression but it was a look so full of love that it lifted my heart. "That's what the world needs," I said to myself, "a lot more open, honest love."

The smile of one dad for his daughter isn't going to change the world on its own but, ultimately, love's the only thing that will.

Ever-loving Lord, thank you seems so small a phrase
yet it's the only one I've got for what I feel.
I'll try to use it more.

James 1:19-20

Everyone should be quick to listen, slow to speak and
slow to become angry, for man's anger does not bring about
the righteous life that God desires.

A little girl said recently, "When your mum's mad with your dad, don't let her brush your hair." A bit of practical wisdom born from experience. I can see the picture clearly. Mum, still a bit uptight with something Dad's done or, more likely, not done, brushing small daughter's hair a bit more vigorously than usual. The victim 'ouching' and 'aahing' with every brush stroke.

Mum, upset, gets a bit aggressive, and daughter becomes the innocent victim. And isn't that the way much of the world works? One country's leaders, angry and upset by the behaviour of another, take strong action – and who suffers? The innocents, caught up in the middle. They've done nothing wrong, they're just in the wrong place at the wrong time.

And when we come down to a personal level, it might be wise to check our feelings when we're angry, and think about whom we're aiming at when we let those feelings loose. Another child said, "Wisdom comes with age, but sometimes age comes on its own."

Long-suffering Lord, it's patience that I need,
but it seems I have to wait for it.

Overleaf:
October Ride, *Watercolour*

Psalm 13:5−6

But I trust in your unfailing love;
my heart rejoices in your salvation.
I will sing to the LORD, for he has been good to me.

Just an ordinary winter shopping day, chilly and wet. Grey cloud. I parked the car in the multi-storey and got into the lift. An elderly couple followed me in and they were the first out at ground floor level. As they walked off in front of me, they each stretched out an arm, feeling for their partner's hand. They didn't have to look, they knew from long practice where it would be. And they walked off, hand-in-hand, grey heads together. Great, I thought.

A few yards further on, a young couple in their early twenties. He had his arm round the girl's neck, gently pulling her towards him. You couldn't have got a bus ticket between them. Again, I thought, great.

And then, walking towards me, a young family. Mum, dad, and a little girl of about three. She was holding mum's and dad's hands and swinging her legs up, back and forwards as they walked. Full of confidence that they wouldn't let her fall.

Four generations, all showing in their different ways their love and trust in each other. It was still a chilly, wet and windy day, but something was giving me a warm glow inside. The world's not all bad is it?

Ever-present, ever-loving Lord,
I only have to open my eyes and you are there.

Matthew 5:37

Simply let your 'Yes' be 'Yes,' and your 'No', 'No'...

We visited Iona, that small historic island off the Scottish coast, bleak but beautiful. It's the place where St Columba landed after sailing from Ireland, about 1,500 years ago, and from there he set out to convert Scotland to the Christian faith. I don't think football had been invented then so I reckon his job wasn't quite as difficult as it would be today.

But when Columba set up his monastery on Iona he told his monks, all 12 of them, each "to live in a room with only one door." Today's Health and Safety people might not be happy with that but it's a challenging idea. Living life up front. Taking whatever comes without running away. No back door to slip through when we don't want to face our problems. Being open and honest in our relationships and welcoming all who come to the door.

And there'd be no back room where we could be in private what we'd never be in public. It means being open in all we do, for others to see. Saying what we mean and sticking to it. Politicians please take note.

A great ideal, much easier to say than work out in life, but living in a room with only one door is about living transparently, without pretending. It's worth a try.

Lord, I open my life to you today without pretence.
Come in.

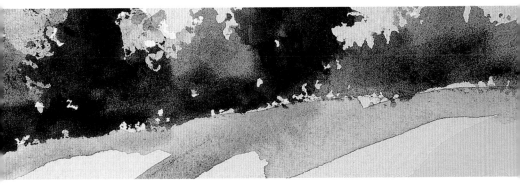

...And whoever wants to be first must be your slave –
just as the Son of Man did not come to be served, but to serve,
and to give his life as a ransom for many.

We have a hairdresser who comes to the house to do Barbara's hair. It's not a luxury, it's just that Barbara can't get to the hairdresser's as easily as she used to. Last time the hairdresser came, she brought her niece with her. She's taking a course in hairdressing at college. She was very enthusiastic about it. We chatted about her training, and what she hoped to do when she'd finished the course. I asked would she be doing hair in people's homes, or in a salon, or even starting her own salon?

One thing she said stuck in my mind: "I don't mind how it turns out; the one thing I want to do is help people feel good about themselves." That's a great ideal, and I reckon it'll make her a good hairdresser, and she'll never want for clients. And whether we're talking about hairdressing or anything else – it's great to make people feel good about themselves.

Life would have a better quality if we all had that ideal firmly in mind, and did what we could to put it into practice. To take the focus off ourselves, and help the folk we're in contact with feel good about themselves. We may not need a college course for that, and if we turned it into reality I reckon we'd feel good about ourselves too.

Servant Lord, give me the grace to see my neighbour
with the love that you see me.

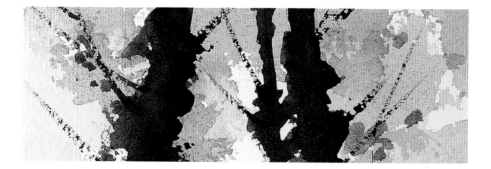

He is like a man building a house, who dug down deep and laid the foundation on rock. When a flood came, the torrent struck that house but could not shake it, because it was well built.

Our neighbour's a professional builder and he's started building a new bungalow in his very spacious garden, with planning permission of course. We're good friends and I'm watching progress with interest. He works to very high standards and has put a lot of thought and planning into it.

I've noticed that with any sort of building work there are times when nothing much seems to be happening, and other times when things develop at great speed. When I mentioned this to Terry he agreed. Then he said, "But, when you think nothing's happening, there's a lot of work going on that you don't see from outside. When you're doing the foundations you've got to think about water supply and sewerage, damp-proofing, insulation and electricity and...oh, so many things." And even before that there's the thought that goes into the plans themselves. The whole of the building will only be as good as the work that's put in on the foundations, and which no-one will ever see.

I reckon that applies to life too. Learning to live with each other and building relationships is a long, slow process. It can't be rushed and what we build together is only as good as the foundations we've put in.

Creative Lord,
help me build my life on your foundations.

Overleaf:
Feeding the Geese, *Watercolour*

47

Deuteronomy 32:7

Remember the days of old;
consider the generations long past.

The other Sunday we went to our village church in Attenborough. There's always a warm welcome there. It's an ancient church – I think there's been some sort of structure on the spot since Saxon times, more than 1,000 years ago – and it was comfortably full. Once we'd found a pew, I started to look around.

One of the things I enjoy looking at in the church is the gargoyles. Now I have to be careful here. Let me make it quite clear that when I say gargoyles I'm definitely not referring to the present congregation who are, on average, several centuries younger than the carvings, and don't look like them anyway. I'm talking about a little group of carved stone characters who look down on us from the top of one of the pillars that hold up an archway. The gargoyles are beautifully carved, but they're caricatures.

They took my mind back through the centuries and I imagined some of the masons getting rid of their frustrations over a difficult overseer by carving a parody of him in a way that would endure for hundreds of years. And then, looking at them, I thought of all the centuries of faith and friendship they'd looked down on. All the joys and sadnesses they could tell us about, and all the strength that this faith and friendship had given to so many to help them cope in their daily lives.

If only the gargoyles could speak.

Lord of the centuries,
give me the ears to hear the whispers of the years,
the rumours of faith,
and the endless prayers of saints.

John 6:11

*Jesus then took the loaves, gave thanks, and distributed
to those who were seated as much as they wanted.
He did the same with the fish.*

You can tell a lot about people by the way they eat their sandwiches. Once it's been cut into manageable halves, or quarters if we have visitors, my wife, Barbara, goes into attack mode. She bites straight into the soft centre, where the filling's the most plentiful. She leaves the crusts till the end, as a sort of penance for the joy of the centre.

I creep up on a sandwich. I nibble away at the crusts first, going all the way round the sandwich, getting rid of the least tasty bits, and saving the pleasure of the filling to the end. Maybe it's left over from my very early days when my mum used to say, "If you can't eat your crusts, you're not hungry enough to want any cake."

It carries through into life. My wife always faces problems head on. Takes them on and deals with them without delay. I tend to work my way into a problem, looking at it from all angles and taking my time, not to shirk it, but trying to find the best angle to tackle it from.

So next time you eat a sandwich – whichever way you like best – thank God for it, and spare a thought for the millions around the world who don't even have the luxury of a crust.

*Lord, help me to take the crusts of life
with the same joy that I bite into the soft centre.*

Colossians 3:23

Whatever you do, work at it with all your heart,
as working for the Lord, not for men...

Granddaughter Claudia, now 11, was painting in my studio. Deep concentration and occasional sighs. She was in another world. Her finished painting was full of feeling, expression and colour. The areas of scribble didn't matter. The picture was alive. I pinned it to the wall and we both stepped back to admire her creation.

Later, I picked up my brush, but nothing I did seemed to work. My drawing was poor, the colours crude, the washes muddy. I seemed to have forgotten everything I'd learned about watercolour over the years. Fellow-sufferers will know what I mean. And the more I tried to put it right the worse it got.

"Ah well," I thought, "I'll put it on one side. Maybe it'll look different in the morning." It did – worse. My frustration and dissatisfaction showed through. Time for my large wastepaper basket. But I paused, then decided to pin my painting next to Claudia's. Hers would remind me of her single-mindedness, and that painting a good picture isn't just about technique. It needs commitment, concentration and, above all, sincerity.

It's the same with people really, especially those we love. No need to pin them to the wall. Just give them your full attention for a while.

Creative Lord, may the life I live today be a picture
coloured in the joy that only you can give.

Matthew 10:29

Are not two sparrows sold for a penny? Yet not one of them will fall to the ground apart from the will of your Father.

I'd filled the bird feeder with a mix of seeds and nuts and was watching through the kitchen window. There are less birds in the garden these days, but there were sparrows squabbling, a blackbird, one lonely starling – where have all the others gone? – and a chaffinch. The collared doves and pigeons had found another takeaway for the morning.

As I watched I suddenly realised that those birds didn't have the faintest idea of who'd put the seed there. They didn't even realise that someone had to put it out. For them, the seed's just there. And they never say thank you. They just eat. My satisfaction comes from seeing them there, and knowing I've done just a tiny bit to help them through another winter's day. And that's all I need.

When you think about it, we humans are the only living creatures in the world who can say "thank you". We may think our family dogs do, but that look in Milli's eye when I give her a Choc Drop is less a "thank you", more a "Have you got another one for me?" expression. So, if we are the only living creatures with enough language to allow us to use the word, let's use it a bit more.

Thank you for reading.

Generous Lord, my gratitude's not always up to scratch.
Forgive, and take the desire for the deed.

Overleaf:
Here Comes Lunch, *Watercolour*

Index of Bible references

The Leprosy Mission

Restoring health, hope and dignity

All the profits from the sale of this book are going to the work of The Leprosy Mission in hospitals and rehabilitation centres in the developing world.

Leprosy is a medical condition affecting millions of people, 90% of whom live in the developing world.

Leprosy causes severe disability and even blindness, if untreated, by attacking nerves under the skin, leading to loss of feeling, paralysis and unfelt injury of the hands, feet and face.

Leprosy can be cured using Multidrug Therapy (MDT) in as little as six months to a year. Since the 1980s over 10 million people have been cured with MDT, but the challenge remains as over 750,000 new cases are still detected each year.

TLM Trading Limited, owned by The Leprosy Mission, seeks to create employment by purchasing goods from rehabilitation centres and craft workshops which employ people affected by leprosy. These goods are sold along with gifts, cards and books to raise funds for TLM.

If you would like information about...
• Our mail order gift catalogue
• The Leprosy Mission's work
• Prayer support
• Supporting The Leprosy Mission financially
• Service overseas with The Leprosy Mission
• Making and amending a will and leaving a legacy to TLM

Contact us on ...
Tel: 0845 166 2253 (local rate, UK only)
Email: enquiries@tlmtrading.com

OR use one of the contact addresses on the right.

Useful addresses

TLM TRADING LIMITED
To buy books, gifts and craft items made by leprosy affected people contact us at...
PO Box 212, Peterborough, PE2 5GD, UK
Tel: 01733 239252 Fax: 01733 239258
Email: enquiries@tlmtrading.com
www.tlmtrading.com

TLM INTERNATIONAL
80 Windmill Road, Brentford,
Middlesex, TW8 0QH, UK.
Tel: 020 8326 6767 Fax: 020 8326 6777
Email: friends@tlmint.org
www.leprosymission.org

TLM ENGLAND AND WALES
Channel Islands and the Isle of Man
Goldhay Way, Orton Goldhay,
Peterborough, PE2 5GZ, UK
Tel: 01733 370505 Fax: 01733 404880
Email: post@tlmew.org.uk
www.leprosymission.org.uk

TLM NORTHERN IRELAND
Lagan House, 2A Queens Road,
Lisburn, BT27 4TZ,
Northern Ireland
Tel: 02892 629500 Fax: 02890 381842
Email: info@tlm-ni.org
www.tlm-ni.org

TLM SCOTLAND
Suite 2, Earlsgate Lodge,
Livilands Lane, Stirling,
Scotland FK8 2BG
Tel: 02890 381937 Fax: 02890 381842
Email: contactus@tlmscotland.org.uk
www.tlmscotland.org.uk

The Leprosy Mission has offices all around the world. Please contact TLM International if you would like contact details for any of the following offices:

Africa Regional Office, Australia, Belgium, Canada, Denmark, Finland, France, Germany, Hungary, India Regional Office, Ireland, Italy, Netherlands, New Zealand, Portugal, South-East Asia Regional Office, South Africa, Spain, Sweden, Switzerland, USA (Assoc Org), Zimbabwe

Shop online at www.tlmtrading.com